"When other people see you as a third-class citizen,
the first thing you need is a belief in yourself and the
knowledge that you have rights. The next thing you need
is a group of friends to fight back with."
—Judith Heumann, from her book *Being Heumann*

To Judith Heumann, thank you —M.C.L.

*To Kayla, for always being there with words of encouragement when
they're needed most* —V.M.

This book was painted using a combination of gouache and digital media.

A portion of Abrams's profits from the sale of this book will be donated to Disability Rights Education & Defense Fund. For more information, visit abramsbooks.com/FightingForYes.

Library of Congress Control Number 2022930628

ISBN 978-1-4197-5560-6

Text © 2022 Maryann Cocca-Leffler
Afterword © 2022 Judith Heumann
Illustrations © 2022 Vivien Mildenberger
Book design by Heather Kelly

Printed and bound in China
10 9 8 7 6 5 4 3 2

Abrams Books for Young Readers are available at special discounts when purchased
in quantity for premiums and promotions as well as fundraising or educational use.
Special editions can also be created to specification. For details,
contact specialsales@abramsbooks.com or the address below.

ABRAMS The Art of Books
195 Broadway, New York, NY 10007
abramsbooks.com

FIGHTING FOR YES!

THE STORY OF DISABILITY RIGHTS ACTIVIST JUDITH HEUMANN

by
MARYANN
COCCA-LEFFLER

illustrated by
VIVIEN
MILDENBERGER

with a note from
JUDITH HEUMANN

Abrams Books for Young Readers • New York

Judy was a bright, talkative little girl
who loved music, books, and visiting
her father's butcher shop.

In 1952, when Judy was five years old, her mother signed her up for kindergarten.

The principal took one look at Judy's wheelchair and said, "NO. Judy is a fire hazard."

Next, they tried the Jewish Day School. That principal said that if Judy learned Hebrew she could enter in September.

Judy took Hebrew classes all summer.

But in the fall, the principal changed his mind. "NO," he said. "It's just not going to work out."

Judy's mother discovered that there were no schools that would accept a girl in a wheelchair. All they were hearing was

NO! NO! NO!

Judy watched her younger brother and the neighborhood kids walk to school. Judy wished that she could go too, but instead she stayed home.

For years, a teacher came to the house for a few hours a week, but for a little girl who loved to read, this was not enough time for learning.

Her mother signed her up for after-school activities, but getting anywhere in a wheelchair was a challenge.

Push . . . bump—
over the curbs to
Hebrew class.

Pull . . . bump, bump—
up the stairs to music lessons.

Lift . . . lug—
down to the basement for Brownies.

On most afternoons, Judy played
with her neighborhood friends who
luckily lived on the same side of
the street. They told Judy all
about their classmates, teachers,
and school activities like gym,
library, and music. More than
anything, Judy wanted to go
to school too.

Finally, after a long search and lots of tests, nine-year-old Judy was accepted to the Health Conservation 21 class at Public School 219 (PS 219). It wasn't the same school that her friends went to, but it was SCHOOL! She was excited and a little nervous. It would be the first time she ever rode a bus or learned in a classroom.

On Judy's first day of school, a bus picked her up. It had a lift and tie-downs for her wheelchair. When she got to her new school, she was rolled into the basement classroom. Inside, there were eight students, all using either wheelchairs or leg braces. This was not the fourth-grade classroom that Judy had imagined. Her classmates were all different ages—some even looked like teenagers or adults. Where were all the kids? Where was the cafeteria and gymnasium that her friends always talked about?

Judy soon learned that the so-called "regular" kids were upstairs. They were expected to learn and go on to high school. The "special-ed" kids were here in the basement, away from everyone. They weren't expected to learn much of anything at all.

But Judy was happy to be going to any school.

Judy felt lucky to have her school friends. More and more, her neighborhood friends were taking the city bus to go places like restaurants or the library. Judy couldn't go to any of these places. Stairs were everywhere, and with no ramps to get in the buildings or lifts on the city bus, Judy was stuck at home.

Judy heard the word **NO** much too often. It just didn't seem fair.

There was one place where Judy felt included: Camp Oakhurst, a summer camp for kids with disabilities. There, Judy and the others had freedom and independence. With ramps and trails, their wheelchairs could go anywhere: to the pool, the dining hall, and even the bathroom.

Judy dreamed that someday the whole world would be like camp, a world that included them.

At fourteen years old, Judy became the first student from PS 219's Health Conservation 21 class to go to high school.

Judy had to travel by bus for an hour and a half every day to a wheelchair-accessible high school.

Though there were a few other kids with disabilities at the school, Judy was nervous. For the first time, she had real exams and real grades. And unlike her small classroom at PS 219, Judy joined a big group of kids, many of whom had never seen a kid in a wheelchair before.

Judy didn't have many friends at the high school and felt out of place. No one seemed to look at her as an average teenage girl.

But Judy worked hard and focused on her studies. Her parents were so proud when they got word that Judy would be receiving a leadership award at her high school graduation.

At graduation, all the students receiving awards were seated on the stage.

Judy's father wheeled her to the front, looking for a ramp.

"She doesn't need to be onstage," said the principal. "Just leave her down here."

Judy's father glared. "My daughter will receive her award on the stage with all the other students!"

Bump, bump . . . up the stairs they went.

The principal followed, directing Judy's father to put her in the back, behind the others . . . out of view. When her name was announced, Judy started to wheel forward, but the principal came to her, making sure she was not seen.

"I belong here," Judy said to herself.
But most of the world still said **NO!**

Judy went on to college and studied to be a teacher. She was happy to be living on campus, but it was hard to get around . . . two steps into her dorm, one step into the bathroom.

Soon, Judy and other students with disabilities formed a group to talk about the barriers they faced every day.

"DON'T PEOPLE WITH DISABILITIES HAVE ANY RIGHTS?"

"HOW CAN WE MAKE UNIVERSITIES MORE ACCESSIBLE?"

It was now the mid-1960s, and college students everywhere were protesting. They wanted an end to the Vietnam War. They marched to support Dr. Martin Luther King Jr. and the civil rights movement.

Judy and her friends knew that disability rights **were** civil rights, and they wanted to work to help make changes. She joined student government and became active in politics.

Her burning passion to make change had begun.

Soon after college graduation, Judy applied for her teaching license.

With a friend's help, Judy made her way to the New York City Board of Education building. The flight of stairs to the door and the out-of-reach buttons in the elevator were the first signs that things might not go well. They didn't.

Three months later, Judy got a letter from the Board of Education telling her **NO!** She would not be getting a teaching license because she could not walk. They considered her a danger to the students.

NO! NO! NO!

Judy was angry. She **was** qualified. She took all the right college classes and passed the oral and written exams. She knew that this was outright discrimination.

Judy decided that she would sue the Board of Education.

No more NOs!

Judy's friend contacted the local media. The next week, an article was published in the *New York Times* about how Judy was being denied a teaching license because of her wheelchair.

Immediately, Judy's phone started ringing. She received calls from civil rights attorneys offering to take her case.

Word spread quickly. Before she knew it, there were articles in newspapers all over the country. Then came letters of support, endorsements, and even an appearance on the *TODAY* show.

On May 26, 1970, Judy sued the New York City Board of Education and WON! Finally, a **YES!**

Then another **YES!** New York passed a law that said people with disabilities would not be prevented from teaching.

Judy was elated, but she knew that her victories were not hers alone. It was only with public support—and the strong voices of fellow activists—that changes could be made. Judy and her friends were determined to keep fighting. They joined together and created Disabled in Action, an organization to fight for the rights of all people with disabilities.

Now twenty-five, Judy was teaching second grade by day.
On nights and weekends, she fought for disability rights.
While reading piles of legal paperwork, Judy noticed a
sentence in Section 504 of the proposed Rehabilitation Act.
She stopped. Was she reading this right? She read it again . . .

No otherwise qualified handicapped individual in the United States . . . shall, solely by reason of his handicap, be excluded from the participation in, be denied the benefits of, or be subjected to discrimination under any program or activity receiving Federal financial assistance . . .

Judy couldn't believe her eyes! This was big!

This meant that if a program or organization received federal funds, people with disabilities had to be included and have equal access.

If Section 504 became law, buildings would be wheelchair accessible, streets would have sidewalk ramps, and buses would have lifts. Judy smiled. Life would be like her childhood summer camp, where everyone with disabilities had freedom and independence.

Judy would do anything to make sure Section 504 became law!

But FIVE years later, Section 504 was still not signed!

It was 1977, and Judy was now working in Washington, D.C., trying to help get 504 passed. But, just like stairs and curbs, the path to becoming law was constantly being blocked.

The government kept delaying signing because organizations complained that it would cost too much money to adapt their buildings for people with disabilities.

Little by little, the wording of the law was being changed and watered down. Disability activists everywhere were tired of waiting. It was time to act!

The American Coalition of Citizens with Disabilities, an organization Judy cofounded, made a public announcement: If the government did **not** sign 504 into law by April 5, 1977, as originally written, there would be nationwide demonstrations.

April 5 arrived, and with no signing in sight, an army of people with disabilities descended on the federal Health, Education, and Welfare (HEW) offices all over the country.

Judy, who was in charge of the San Francisco demonstration, watched with pride as the plaza filled with hundreds of supporters. The crowd was diverse—people in wheelchairs, those with canes and braces, parents of disabled children, civil rights leaders, and church groups were all there to support the cause.

Judy rolled up to the microphone and looked out into the growing crowd. With a lump in her throat and a **SIGN 504!** sticker on her jacket, she began to speak.

"When they are signed, the regulations for Section 504 will be a historic and monumental first step toward knocking down the walls that stop us, people with disabilities, from being full and equal participants in society."

A chant erupted from the crowd . . .

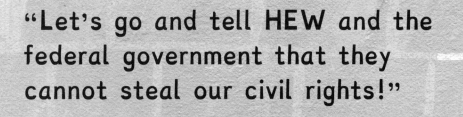

"Let's go and tell HEW and the federal government that they cannot steal our civil rights!"

Judy turned her wheelchair and headed to the entrance of the federal building. The crowd followed. More than one hundred demonstrators with disabilities made their way to the government offices on the fourth floor.

They vowed **NOT** to leave until 504 was signed! The 504 Sit-in had begun!

While protests in other cities ended the same day they began, San Francisco stayed strong. Time ticked on. Minutes became hours. Hours became days. Local and national organizations supported their cause by bringing in medicine, food, mattresses, blankets, and other necessities.

The government tried to force them out by shutting off the hot water and blocking the phone lines.

The locked-in protesters were not deterred. They communicated with Washington, D.C., and the national media through pay phones in the hallway and kept the supporters in the plaza updated by using sign language through the windows.

They slept on the floor,
ate hot-dog soup, "showered"
in the sink, and supported each other
through song and prayer. The protesters
would occupy the building until 504 was signed, no
matter how long it took. They were strong and proud
and determined to be heard.

Finally, on April 28, 1977, the government listened.

After five years, three presidential administrations, nationwide demonstrations, a twenty-four-day takeover of the federal building in San Francisco, and more **NOs** than Judy could count . . .

Section 504 was signed!

"YES! YES! YES!"

YES!
YES!
YES!
YES!
SIGN 504
WE WILL WAIT NO MORE!
EQUAL OPPORTUNITY 504!
504!
504

Dear Reader
A NOTE FROM JUDITH HEUMANN

My name is Judy. Thank you for taking the time to read this book about my life growing up with a disability. There were many times in my life when not being able to walk was a problem. But I have learned over the years that many of those problems can be fixed.

You have learned by reading this book about problems I faced and how my friends and I were able to fix them. We worked together to fix problems that were making it hard for us to be a part of our communities. One of those problems is discrimination.

Disabled people sometimes experience discrimination. An example of discrimination is when I was not allowed to go to school because I use a wheelchair. Discrimination may make us feel upset or angry. It feels like the world is telling us **NO**.

We are still fighting for **YES** every single day. I have a physical disability and can't walk. I have friends who have other disabilities. For example, they are blind or deaf, or have learning disabilities, diabetes, depression, or anxiety. Some people experience discrimination because they are disabled and also because of their race, religion, or other parts of who they are. We all work together to make our lives better.

I enjoy working with other people. Fixing problems together helps us feel that we are not alone. It's also important to work with people who are different from you so you can learn how to make our world a better place for everyone.

Today, I use a motorized wheelchair. When I was young, it had not been invented yet. Now I can go to many places by myself. I no longer have to be pulled up stairs and over sidewalk curbs. Now, many buildings have ramps and sidewalks have curb cuts that make it easier for me to get around in my wheelchair. But many of my friends live in homes that have steps and no ramps. There is much more work that needs to be done.

We—disabled and non-disabled people—are changing the world. Reading this book is a great way to learn about how you can fix problems, like I did. How will you start fighting for **YES**? Are there things you think need to change? Do you or any of your friends experience discrimination? Talk about your feelings to find ways you can work together. Fighting for **YES** starts with **YOU**!

Author's Note

Judith Heumann was born on December 18, 1947, to Ilse and Werner Heumann in Brooklyn, New York, during the height of the polio epidemic. When Judy was eighteen months old, she contracted polio. After she recovered, she was unable to walk and had limited use of her hands and arms.

The doctor recommended that Judy be placed in an institution, where she would be cared for away from her family. Her parents said **NO**. They would not be separated from their child, and they took Judy home.

From a young age, Judy used a wheelchair and, because of her disability, has faced discrimination her whole life. Early on, she was not allowed to attend school and had to stay at home.

At age nine, after being placed on a waiting list and having her abilities evaluated, Judy was finally allowed to attend the Health Conservation 21 class in a public school outside of her neighborhood. She traveled three hours a day in a wheelchair-accessible bus to get to and from school, where her classroom was in the basement, segregated from the rest of the school. Her classmates, ages six to twenty-one, all had disabilities.

Judy got a glimpse of what life **could** be like for people with disabilities at Camp Oakhurst and later at Camp Jened, where she spent many years as a counselor. The freedom and independence she felt there spurred her passion for change.

After high school, Judy went on to Long Island University (LIU), where she studied to be a teacher. Though highly qualified, the New York City Board of Education denied her a teaching license. They considered her "a danger to the students."

Judy sued the board. Her lawsuit was the first disability civil rights case ever filed in a federal court. After the court ordered another medical exam, which she passed, Judy was awarded her teaching license, but her excitement was short-lived. No one would hire her because most schools did not have access for a wheelchair. She almost gave up, but finally she got a teaching job at her old school, PS 219.

From then on, Judy became an advocate for the disabled community. She was the first president of Disabled in Action, a civil rights organization run by and for people with disabilities. While still teaching, she kept a close eye on Section 504 of the proposed Rehabilitation Act. As a law, it would give people with disabilities

equal rights and accessibility to federally funded public buildings, streets, and transportation.

She left teaching to continue her education, and in 1974, Judy took a legislative assistant position in Washington, D.C., where she championed disability issues, including employment and education for people with disabilities. She was also on a team working on Section 504 of the Rehabilitation Act of 1973. The 504 amendment had been languishing for five years, jumping from one committee to the next, waiting to be signed.

On April 5, 1977, protesters assembled at the federal offices of the Department of Health, Education, and Welfare (HEW) all over the country to push for the signing of Section 504, unchanged. Judy led the San Francisco protest with help from Kitty Cone, Mary Jane Owen, Ed Roberts, and many other activists. While all the other protests ended that day, Judy and more than 100 people with disabilities took over the HEW offices and vowed to stay there until 504 was signed. It was called the 504 Sit-in.

Though the government tried to impede their efforts, many different organizations joined in support, including the Black Panthers, who brought in food; the Salvation Army, who set up beds; and a host of other organizations and churches.

About twenty days after the sit-in began, a thirty-four-person delegation, including Judy, headed to Washington, D.C., to put pressure on Congress to act.

After days of meetings and rallies, they had finally gained congressional support.

On April 28, 1977, the twenty-fourth day of the sit-in, Section 504 was signed, unchanged. The 504 Sit-in was the longest nonviolent occupation of a federal building in United States history. On April 30, the victorious protesters left the federal building for the last time.

Judith Heumann's advocacy, and that of many other people, did not end with the signing of 504. Judy went on to make certain that the law was enforced. Many did not want to comply with the law because of the costs. It took years for public buildings, schools, buses, trains, and sidewalks to become accessible to people with disabilities.

Throughout the 1980s, Judy—along with others in the disability community—fought for the expansion of 504, which formed the basis for the American Disabilities Act (ADA).

The ADA is a civil rights law that prohibits people with disabilities from being discriminated against in all areas of life, including jobs and schools. It expanded accessibility to include all privately owned buildings such as theaters, restaurants, and work environments.

Finally, on July 26, 1990, President George H.W. Bush signed the American Disabilities Act into law with these words:

"Let the shameful wall of exclusion finally come tumbling down."

The ADA is the most comprehensive civil rights legislation for disabilities in the world, and there is no doubt that the fight for 504 paved the way.

Judy went on to serve in both the Clinton and Obama administrations as an advocate for people with disabilities. She continues to champion disability rights in the United States and around the world.

SECTION 504 TODAY

No otherwise qualified individual with a disability in the United States, as defined in Section 705 (20) of this title, shall, solely by reason of his or her disability, be excluded from the participation in, be denied the benefits of, or be subjected to discrimination under any program or activity receiving Federal financial assistance or under any program or activity conducted by any Executive agency . . .

Selected Sources

BOOKS

Heumann, Judith, with Kristin Joiner. *Being Heumann: An Unrepentant Memoir of a Disability Rights Activist*. Boston: Beacon Press, 2020.

Longmore, Paul K., and Lauri Umansky, eds. *The New Disability History*. New York: New York University Press, 2001.

VIDEOS/MOVIES

Heumann, Judith. *Our Fight for Disability Rights—And Why We're Not Done Yet*. TEDxMidAtlantic, October 2016. See www.ted.com/talks/judith_heumann_our_fight_for_disability_rights_and_why_we_re_not_done_yet?language=en.

The Power of 504. See www.vimeo.com/channels/504sitin.

Newnham, Nicole, and Jim LeBrect, dirs. *Crip Camp: A Disability Revolution*. Higher Ground Productions, 2020. See cripcamp.com.

WEBSITES

Disability Rights Education and Defense Fund. "504 Sit-in 20th Anniversary." See dredf.org/504-sit-in-20th-anniversary.

Polio Place. "Judith Ellen Heumann." February 2012. See www.polioplace.org/people/judith-e-heumann.

Shoot, Britta. "The 1977 Disability Rights Protest That Broke Records and Changed Laws." Atlas Obscura, November 9, 2017. See www.atlasobscura.com/articles/504-sit-in-san-francisco-1977-disability-rights-advocacy.

US Department of Labor. "Rehabilitation Act of 1973" See www.dol.gov/agencies/oasam/centers-offices/civil-rights-center/statutes/section-504-rehabilitation-act-of-1973.

Notes

"When they are signed, the regulations for Section 504 . . ." Judith Heumann with Kristin Joiner, *Being Heumann: An Unrepentant Memoir of a Disability Rights Activist*. (Boston: Beacon Press, 2020), 91.

"Let's go and tell HEW and the federal government that they cannot steal our civil rights!" Heumann, 93.

"Let the shameful wall of exclusion finally come tumbling down." President George H. W. Bush at the signing of the Americans with Disabilities Act, July 26, 1990.

"When other people see you as a third-class citizen, the first thing you need is a belief in yourself and the knowledge that you have rights. The next thing you need is a group of friends to fight back with." Heumann, 64.